CASTLES OF NORTHUMBERLAND

PHOTOGRAPHY
GRAEME PEACOCK

TEXT
PAUL FRODSHAM

NORTHERN
HERITAGE

Northern Heritage,
Units 7&8 New Kennels, Blagdon Estate, Seaton Burn,
Newcastle upon Tyne NE13 6DB
Telephone: 01670 789 940
www.northern-heritage.co.uk

ISBN No.978-0-9544777-9-0

Printed and bound in China by 1010 Printing International Limited.

British Library Cataloguing in Publishing Data
A catalogue record for this book is available from the British Library.

Also available in this series:

Places featured in this book are managed and interpreted for the public
by a combination of agencies including English Heritage, the National
Trust, local authorities, conservation charities and private landowners.
When visiting them, please treat them with respect and avoid damaging
ancient monuments (eg by climbing on walls) or disturbing natural
habitats. Details of opening times, admission charges etc are available from
tourist information centres.

GRAEME PEACOCK

Graeme Peacock is one of the best known and
highly regarded photographers of landscapes and
architecture in the North of England. A former Town
Planner, born 'n bred on Tyneside, Graeme has for
over 20 years built up a stock in excess of 49,000
stunning colour images of our region. Regular
clients include The National Trust, English Heritage,
Ordnance Survey and The Royal Mail. To see more
Graeme Peacock images visit his website
www.graeme-peacock.com

INTRODUCTION

The word 'castle' has been applied to a variety of sites in Northumberland, including prehistoric hillforts, Roman forts, a variety of medieval fortified houses and towers, and even follies of the 18th and 19th centuries. True castles, however, of which Northumberland has about twenty, are the great medieval fortresses of the Norman barons and their descendents. The turbulent nature of the Anglo-Scottish border throughout medieval times ensured that many of these remained in service for 500 years after the Norman Conquest. Not without good reason has Northumberland been labelled 'England's Castle County'.

The earliest castles, built by barons to whom William the Conqueror granted land after 1066, were 'motte and baileys', consisting of an earthen mound topped with a timber tower, all enclosed within a bailey surrounded by a timber palisade. In Northumberland, Elsdon is a classic example of a motte and bailey, abandoned before there was an opportunity to develop it further. Most motte and baileys were eventually given strong, stone curtain walls in place of earth and timber defences, with towers often added at intervals along the walls. In the mid 12th century, stone keeps were introduced. These could be strong towers (eg Bamburgh and Norham) or 'shell keeps' surrounding open courtyards (eg Alnwick). Massive, often elaborate gatehouses were also added to many castles, often with a second, outer gatehouse known as a barbican. Barbicans gave extra protection to the entrance as well as providing very visible statements of power through which all visitors would have to pass. Some later castles (eg Dunstanburgh) combined gatehouse and keep within a single massive structure, while others adopted completely new forms such as the quadrangular castle (eg Chillingham).

In addition to these great castles, a bewildering array of secondary, but still impressive, defended houses and towers were built by wealthy landowners. These are generally distinguished from the great castles by the fact that they are usually contained beneath a single roof. Smaller still are the 'bastles', or defended farmhouses, of which as many as 500 may have been built throughout Northumberland during the late 16th and early 17th centuries.

As new forms of heavy artillery were introduced, castles became increasingly susceptible to bombardment and many were badly damaged and never brought back into effective service. After the Union of the Crowns in 1603, there was no longer the need for so many castles in the region, and while some were adapted as grand houses, many were simply abandoned and became convenient sources of building stone for new projects.

Although their ruins can appear mysterious, Northumberland's great castles have many documented links with known historical figures and events and have played key roles in British history. They have been painted by Canaletto and Turner, written about by Shakespeare and Walter Scott, and now form some of the finest jewels in the very rich crown that is Northumberland's historic environment. This collection of Graeme Peacock's excellent photographs represents an ideal souvenir for anyone fortunate enough to have visited one or more of the featured sites, and should also be of value to anyone with an interest in 'England's Castle County'.

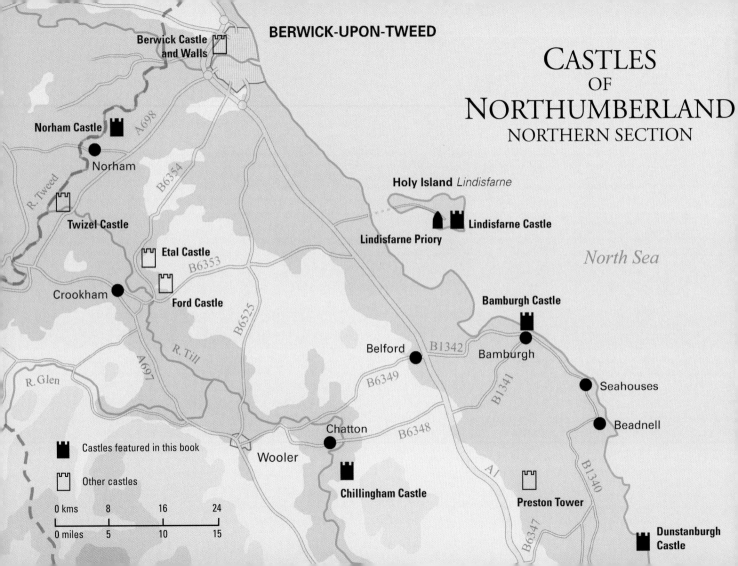

BERWICK-UPON-TWEED

Berwick Castle
and Walls

CASTLES
OF
NORTHUMBERLAND
NORTHERN SECTION

Norham Castle

Norham

R. Tweed

A698

B6354

Twizel Castle

Etal Castle

B6353

Crookham

Ford Castle

Holy Island *Lindisfarne*

Lindisfarne Castle

Lindisfarne Priory

North Sea

B6525

R. Till

R. Glen

A697

A697

Bamburgh Castle

Belford

B1342

Bamburgh

B6349

B1341

Seahouses

B6348

Beadnell

Chatton

Wooler

Chillingham Castle

A1

Preston Tower

B1340

B6347

Dunstanburgh
Castle

■ Castles featured in this book

▢ Other castles

| 0 kms | 8 | 16 | 24 |

| 0 miles | 5 | 10 | 15 |

The keep, Norham Castle.

Norham Castle guards a strategic crossing point of the Tweed on an ancient cross-border route. From medieval times until the mid 19th century, Norhamshire was not in Northumberland, but was part of the County Palatinate of Durham, controlled by the Bishops of Durham. The first castle here, a timber motte and bailey, was built in about 1121. Norham suffered much damage at the hands of the Scots, being taken twice during the 1130s, but was rebuilt in stone in the later 12th century after which it withstood three major sieges between 1215 and 1319. It was eventually taken by the Scots in 1327, but was soon returned as part of a treaty. Prior to the Battle of Flodden in 1513, it was again taken by the Scots, under James IV, but only after two months of bombardment. The castle was repaired after Flodden, but was reported as being in poor repair by the late 16th century and was not maintained after the Union of the Crowns. The remains visible today date from various phases of its history: the massive red sandstone keep dates originally from the 12th century but was substantially enlarged (from three to five stories) in the 1420s.

Norham Castle towers above the River Tweed.

Lindisfarne (Holy Island) has played a key role in Northumbrian history, but this is due to its monastery rather than its castle. The original monastery, founded by St Aidan in 635, was sacked by Vikings in 793 and abandoned in 875. Lindisfarne Priory was founded on the same site in 1083 by William of St Calais, Bishop of Durham, and survived until the Dissolution in1537. The castle, occupying a spectacular position on the highest point of the island, an outcrop of the Whin Sill known as Beblowe Crag, is much later – it was built in 1550, partly using stone plundered form the abandoned Priory. Its architecture incorporates two lines of gun emplacements, but these saw little service as the site was of no great strategic importance after the Union of the Crowns. Nevertheless, the castle was garrisoned until 1819, after which it became a coastguard station until the late 19th century when it was purchased by Edward Hudson, owner of Country Life Magazine. He employed Edward Lutyens to transform the remains of the austere old fort into a comfortable home, which he did brilliantly. Today the site is owned by the National Trust.

Lindisfarne Castle and harbour with Bamburgh Castle and the Farne Islands on the horizon.

St Aidan's statue and Lindisfarne Castle.

Castle Gardens, Lindisfarne.

Bamburgh Castle is wonderfully sited high above the coast on an outcrop of the Whin Sill. The site was probably first defended as a hillfort in late prehistoric times, and may have been occupied ever since. It was taken by Ida in 547, and from here the great Anglian Kingdom of Northumbria, soon to extend from the Humber to the Forth, was born. After the Viking invasions of the late 9th century, Northumbria continued to be ruled by earls based at Bamburgh. The castle was built by the Normans in the late 11th century, and the impressive keep dates from the mid 12th century. Over subsequent centuries, Bamburgh gradually lost power and influence to Alnwick, and after being badly damaged in a siege of 1464 lay in a state of disrepair for two and a half centuries. Eventually, in 1704, it was purchased by Lord Crewe (Bishop of Durham), leading to much repair work during the 18th century when it functioned as a base for a variety of charitable institutions including a school and a library. In 1894, the castle was bought by Lord Armstrong who added several new structures to the ancient ruins, most notably the grand King's Hall on the site of the 14th-century great hall.

*Above: **Bamburgh Castle at night.***
*Right: **Bamburgh Castle from Harkness Rocks.***

Bamburgh Castle and village under a snowy mantle.

Bamburgh Castle from Bamburgh village.

Chillingham is a superb example of a mid 14th-century castle. It is very different from earlier, Norman castles, being roughly square in plan with a curtain wall surrounding a central courtyard and a substantial tower in each corner. Internal buildings are arranged against the inner face of the curtain wall, linking the towers. In the early 17th century, after the Union of the Crowns when military strength was no longer the priority, an elaborate entrance façade was added to the north wall. Many other modifications followed, but sadly the castle lay unoccupied for several decades during the 20th century, allowing decay to set in. Fortunately, much conservation work has been completed since the present owner, Sir Humphrey Wakefield, took over in the 1980s. Today, the castle owes much of its fame to the herd of 'wild' white cattle which has existed in its grounds since the 13th century. Its gardens were designed in the 1820s by Sir Jeffry Wyatville, famous for his work at Windsor Castle.

Left: **The Walled Garden, Chillingham Castle.**

The dramatic ruins of Dunstanburgh Castle occupy an outcrop of dolerite overlooking Embleton Bay. Like Bamburgh, Dunstanburgh was probably a prehistoric hillfort, but there the comparison ends. In complete contrast to Bamburgh, Dunstanburgh has no evidence of early medieval, or even Norman occupation, having not been built until about 1315. In terms of its internal area, it is the largest castle in Northumberland at 4.5 hectares, but it played no great role in Northumbrian history. It was much fought over during the Wars of the Roses, changing hands five times and suffering so much bombardment that it was in ruins by the end of this period of conflict in 1485. It was abandoned by the mid 16th century and never reoccupied. Today's ruins owe their instantly recognisable appearance to the great three-storeyed gatehouse with its distinctive twin towers rising to five storeys. This gatehouse contained the great hall and all the castle's main rooms. The ruins of the Lilburn Tower, on the west side of the castle, are also mightily impressive.

Dunstanburgh Castle from Embleton Bay.

View from the gatehouse, Dunstanburgh Castle.

The gatehouse, Dunstanburgh Castle.

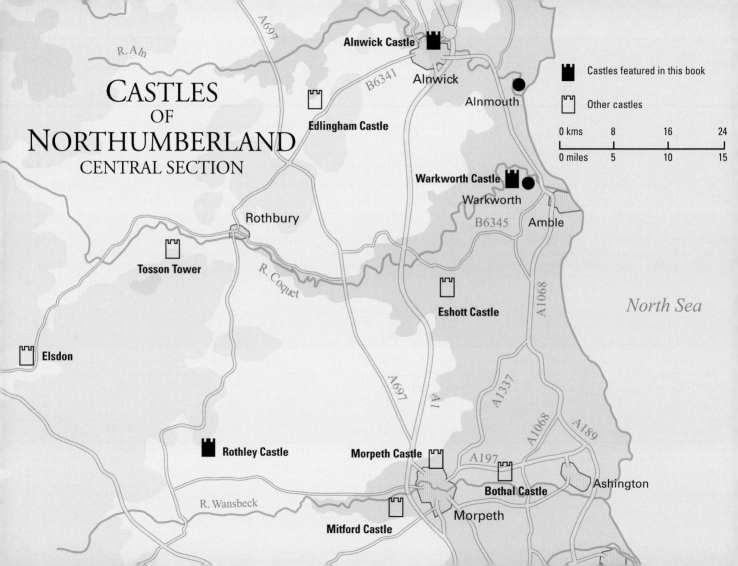

CASTLES
OF
NORTHUMBERLAND
CENTRAL SECTION

R. Aln

A697

B6341

Alnwick Castle

Alnwick

Alnmouth

■ Castles featured in this book

▢ Other castles

0 kms   8   16   24

0 miles   5   10   15

Edlingham Castle

Warkworth Castle

Warkworth

B6345

Amble

North Sea

A1068

Rothbury

Tosson Tower

R. Coquet

Eshott Castle

A697

A1

A1337

A1068

A189

Elsdon

Rothley Castle

Morpeth Castle

A197

Ashington

Bothal Castle

R. Wansbeck

Mitford Castle

Morpeth

Alnwick Castle has been termed 'The Windsor of the North', but such a comparison is demeaning. Alnwick is a magnificent castle in its own right, in a superb landscape setting and with a fascinating history of its own. Originally a timber motte and bailey in a strong natural position above the Aln, it was begun by one of William the Conquerer's barons, Yvo de Vescy, in 1096. The stone castle, consisting of the great keep with its central courtyard, and two surrounding baileys, was built in the mid 12th century. In 1309 the castle was purchased by the Yorkshire-based Henry de Percy. The Percy family was destined to become one of the most powerful families in northern England, and Alnwick Castle was developed as an appropriately grand family seat. The magnificent gatehouse and barbican were built in the early 14th century, and the castle had achieved pretty much its present form by 1350.

The male Percy line died out, along with the earldom, in 1670, but Sir Hugh Smithson, who married into the family in the mid 18th century and assumed the Percy name, was created Duke of Northumberland for services to George III. He undertook much reconstruction work on the castle and oversaw the landscaping of the grounds by Capability Brown. The fourth Duke spent £1/4 million on building work and refurbishment in the mid 19th century, employing the best available Italian designers and craftsmen to create the sumptuous Italian state rooms. Today, Alnwick Castle is home to the twelfth Duke of Northumberland and is the base from which the extensive Northumberland Estates are managed.

Recent work on the Castle Gardens have turned these into a popular tourist attraction in their own right, and the castle has achieved fame with a new generation through its role as Hogwarts in the Harry Potter films. Alnwick Castle has been one of the most important places in Northumberland for nearly a thousand years, and, together with its grounds and gardens, surely ranks today as one of this nation's most exquisite historic sites.

Alnwick Castle from the Pastures.

Above: **The gatehouse, Alnwick town.**
Left: **The barbican and gatehouse, Alnwick Castle.**

Looking down to the River Aln from the battlements, Alnwick Castle.

The lion standing proud on the Lion Bridge, Alnwick.

The Treehouse, Alnwick Castle Gardens.

Shakespeare called it a 'worm-eaten hold of rugged stone', but for today's visitor Warkworth Castle represents everything a ruined medieval castle should be. Its neatly consolidated yet still romantic ruins occupy a commanding position above a wooded bend in the Coquet. It is not known exactly when the first castle, presumably a timber motte and bailey, was built here, but the first stone castle was built by Henry, Earl of Northumberland and son of King David I of Scotland, in the mid 12th century. Owned by the Percys from 1332, Warkworth endured a complex and often violent history, featuring regularly in Anglo-Scottish border conflict and undergoing a series of modifications through until the late 14th century.

Warkworth Castle from the west.

The magnificent great keep, built on the site of an earlier keep following the Scottish invasion of 1383/4, is Warkworth's most imposing feature. It combined great military strength with comfortable accommodation, and must have been amongst the grandest structures to be seen in 15th century Britain. The castle was battered during the Civil War, after which it became a convenient quarry for those seeking building material for projects elsewhere.

Warkworth Castle from the River Coquet.

Looking towards Warkworth Castle from Warkworth village.

Warkworth Castle gatehouse.

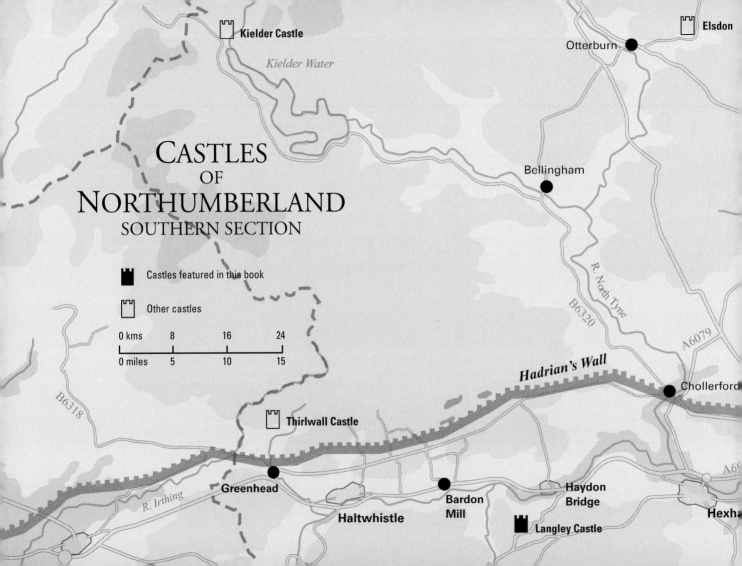

CASTLES
OF
NORTHUMBERLAND
SOUTHERN SECTION

Kielder Castle

Kielder Water

Elsdon

Otterburn

Bellingham

R. North Tyne

B6320

A6079

■ Castles featured in this book

⌂ Other castles

0 kms	8	16	24
0 miles	5	10	15

Hadrian's Wall

Chollerford

B6318

Thirlwall Castle

R. Irthing

Greenhead

Haltwhistle

Bardon Mill

Haydon Bridge

Hexha

A6

Langley Castle

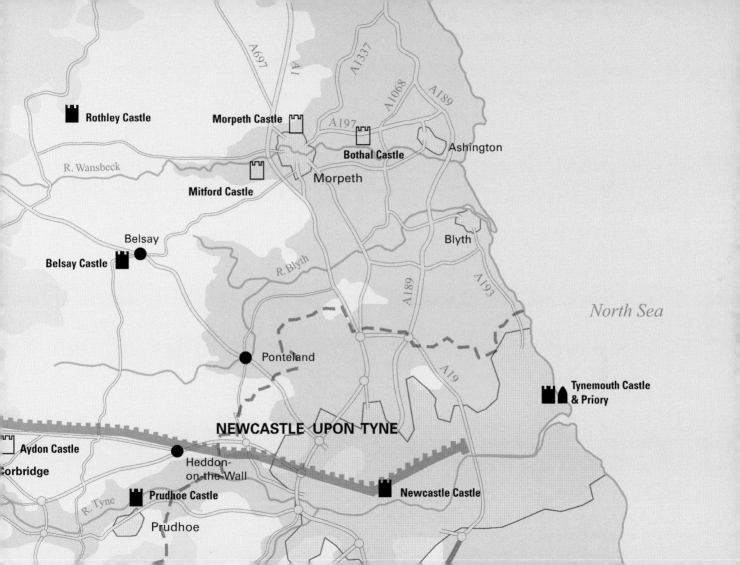

R othley Castle is by some way the latest structure featured in this book. Although anyone looking at these photographs might reasonably assume otherwise, this 'castle' is actually a folly dating from the 1750s. It was built at a dramatic viewpoint as part of Sir Walter Calverley Blackett's grand scheme to landscape parts of his estate at Wallington, and should not be mistaken for a 'genuine' castle.

Rothley Castle.

Springtime, Belsay Castle.

Belsay Castle Gardens.

The origins of Belsay Castle are not known, but must predate the construction of the tower-house, the oldest visible element of the site today, in about 1370. This distinctive and imposing tower incorporates four corner turrets, one of which is larger than the others. In 1614, the now roofless manor-house was added to the tower. This may have destroyed some earlier buildings, but now complements the ancient tower beautifully. The magnificent Belsay Hall, dating from the early 19th century, lies 300m east of the castle. The gardens at Belsay, dating from the 18th century onwards, are another important element of this extraordinary and fascinating place.

An imposing tower-house, largely remodelled in the mid 14th century by Sir Thomas de Lucy to provide protection against Scottish raids, Langley was then destroyed by the English! It was attacked in 1405 by Henry IV as part of his campaign to put down a rebellion led by Archbishop Scrope, after which the structure seems to have lain abandoned until the 19th century when it was restored from a ruined shell to its current impressive form. In contrast to its violent past, it functions today as a peaceful and very attractive hotel which happily welcomes both English and Scottish guests.

Langley Castle at night.

Prudhoe Castle.

Prudhoe Castle is strongly sited on a hill overlooking the Tyne. Built by the Umphravilles, who came to England alongside William the Conquerer, it probably began life as a late 11th-century timber motte and bailey, but was built in stone by the mid twelfth century and was strong enough to repel a couple of sieges by William the Lion in 1173 and 1174. Prudhoe was acquired by the Percys in 1381, and, other than a couple of periods during which it was confiscated by the Crown, has remained in Percy ownership ever since. Prudhoe's gatehouse, of early 12th-century date with later additions and alterations, is considered one of the finest surviving examples in Britain. In contrast, the keep is one of our smallest rectangular keeps, but is strongly built with walls three metres thick: it probably dates from the 1170s. An attractive early 19th-century house, incorporating much recycled medieval masonry, stands within the castle.

Winter view of Prudhoe Castle.

Prudhoe Castle.

The medieval castle, after which Newcastle is named, occupies the site of the Roman fort of *Pons Aelius.* It has been much damaged by more recent development, notably the construction of the railway in Victorian times, so that its original appearance is now difficult to appreciate. Little is known of the original Norman castle. The magnificent keep dates from a period of rebuilding in the 1170s, although its battlements are 19th-century additions.

Above: **The medieval town walls, Newcastle.**
Right: **The castle keep and the spire of St Nicholas' Cathedral.**

The Black Gate, Newcastle.

The building known as the Black Gate was constructed in about 1250 as a barbican outside the castle's north gate, incorporating a portcullis and drawbridge. The distinctive appearance of the Black Gate today results from the addition of an early 17th-century brick house onto the original structure's two lower floors.

L ocated on a promontory overlooking the sea, Tynemouth Castle occupies a position similar in many ways to those of Bamburgh and Dunstanburgh. Like them, the site seems to have first been fortified as a hillfort in pre-Roman times. The monastery at Tynemouth may have been founded as early as the mid 7th century, and was certainly here by 800. It was sacked by the Vikings in 875, but restored in the 11th century after which it survived until the Dissolution, being finally abandoned in 1539.

Above: **The Priory and North Pier, Tynemouth.**
Left: **Tynemouth Castle.**

Medieval defences surrounded both the monastery and the fort: in combination with the natural defences of the site these made Tynemouth one of the best defended of all Northumberland's medieval castles. The massive gatehouse that survives today is of early 15th-century date. After the Dissolution, the fort was maintained and garrisoned, but sadly, due to a combination of later building work and natural erosion of the cliffs, much medieval masonry has been lost and the castle ruins do not approach those of the adjacent priory in terms of architectural splendour.

Tynemouth Castle.

Tynemouth Priory from the castle.